AF373472

WHY DON'T SKELETONS FIGHT EACH OTHER?

They don't have the guts.

WHY WAS THE COLOR GREEN
NOTORIOUSLY SINGLE?

IT WAS ALWAYS SO JADED.

WHAT'S THE NAME OF A VERY POLITE,
EUROPEAN BODY OF WATER?

MERCI.

Q: WHY DID THE FOOTBALL COACH GO TO THE BANK?

A: TO GET HIS QUARTER BACK.

Q: AIR USED TO BE FREE AT THE GAS STATION, NOW IT COSTS YOU WANT TO KNOW WHY?

A: INFLATION.

IMAGINE IF YOU WALKED INTO A BAR AND THERE WAS A LONG LINE OF PEOPLE WAITING TO TAKE A SWING AT YOU. THAT'S THE PUNCH LINE.

Q: WHAT DO SPRINTERS EAT BEFORE A RACE?

A: NOTHING, THEY FAST!

Q: WHY DO MELONS HAVE WEDDINGS?

A: BECAUSE THEY CANTALOUPE!

Q: HOW DO CELEBRITIES STAY COOL?

A: THEY HAVE MANY FANS.

HOW MANY APPLES GROW ON A TREE?
ALL OF THEM!
WHAT ROCK GROUP HAS FOUR MEN THAT DON'T SING?
MOUNT RUSHMORE.

A GUY GOES TO HIS DOCTOR BECAUSE HE CAN SEE INTO THE FUTURE. THE DOCTOR ASKS HIM, "HOW LONG HAVE YOU SUFFERED FROM THAT CONDITION?"

THE GUY TELLS HIM, "SINCE NEXT MONDAY."

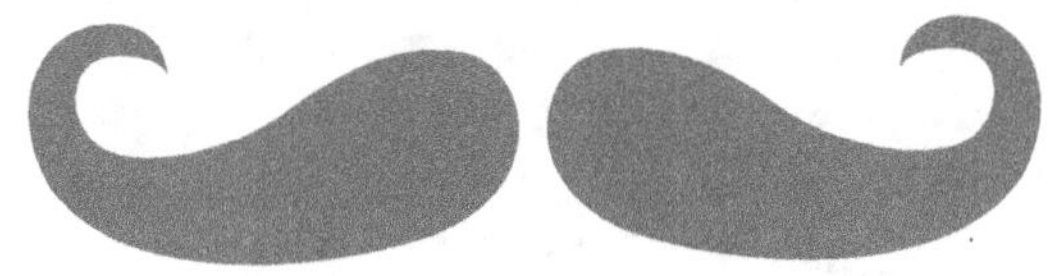

WHEN I WAS A KID, MY MOTHER TOLD ME I COULD BE ANYONE I WANTED TO BE.

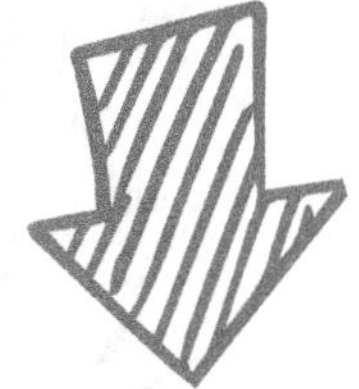

TURNS OUT, IDENTITY THEFT IS A CRIME.

HOW DOES MOSES MAKE HIS COFFEE?

HEBREWS IT.

I'M STARTING A NEW DATING
SERVICE IN PRAGUE.

IT'S CALLED CZECH-MATE.

WHY DID THE COACH GO TO
THE BANK?

TO GET HIS QUARTERBACK.

Q: WHY CAN'T A LEOPARD HIDE?

A: HE'S ALWAYS SPOTTED.

Q: WHAT DO YOU CALL LETTERS THAT WENT FOR A SWIM?

A: ALPHAWETICAL.

I TRIED TO GET A SMART CAR THE OTHER DAY BUT THEY SOLD OUT TOO FAST. WHY? I GUESS I'M JUST A BIT SLOW.

Q: WHAT DO YOU CALL A FACTORY THAT SELLS PASSABLE PRODUCTS?

A: A SATISFACTORY!

Q: WHY DID THE INVISIBLE MAN TURN DOWN THE JOB OFFER?

A: HE COULDN'T SEE HIMSELF DOING IT!

Q: WANT TO HEAR A JOKE ABOUT CONSTRUCTION?

A: I'M STILL WORKING ON IT!

WHY IS IT A BAD IDEA TO IRON YOUR FOUR-LEAF CLOVER?
CAUSE YOU SHOULDN'T PRESS YOUR LUCK.
A CHEESE FACTORY EXPLODED IN FRANCE.
DA BRIE IS EVERYWHERE!

WHAT'S THE DIFFERENCE BETWEEN A POORLY DRESSED MAN ON A TRICYCLE AND A WELL-DRESSED MAN ON A BICYCLE?

ATTIRE!

I CAN'T TAKE MY DOG TO THE POND ANYMORE BECAUSE THE DUCKS KEEP ATTACKING HIM.

THAT'S WHAT I GET FOR BUYING A PURE BREAD DOG.

WHY IS PETER PAN
ALWAYS FLYING?

BECAUSE HE
NEVERLANDS.

I WANT TO MAKE A BRIEF JOKE,

BUT IT'S A LITTLE CHEESY.

WHAT HAPPENS WHEN YOU GO TO
THE BATHROOM IN FRANCE?

EUROPEAN.

Q: HOW CAN YOU TELL THAT SANTA IS REAL?

A: YOU CAN SENSE HIS PRESENTS WHENEVER HE COMES.

WHAT DID THE LATE TOMATO SAY TO THE OTHER TOMATOES?

DON'T WORRY I'LL KETCHUP.

I USED TO HATE FACIAL HAIR, BUT THEN IT GREW ON ME.

WHAT'S EVERY ELF'S FAVORITE TYPE OF MUSIC? IT'S WRAP.

DEAR MATH, IT'S TIME TO GROW UP AND SOLVE YOUR OWN PROBLEMS.

I GAVE AWAY ALL MY USED BATTERIES TODAY. FREE OF CHARGE!

WHAT DO COWS MOST LIKE TO READ?
CATTLE-LOGS.
WHAT DOES SANTA LOVES TO EAT FOR BREAKFAST?
THE FROSTED FLAKES.

WHAT OTHER NAME CAN YOU CALL THE LITTLE HELPERS BELONGING TO SANTA?

THE SUBORDINATE CLAUSES.

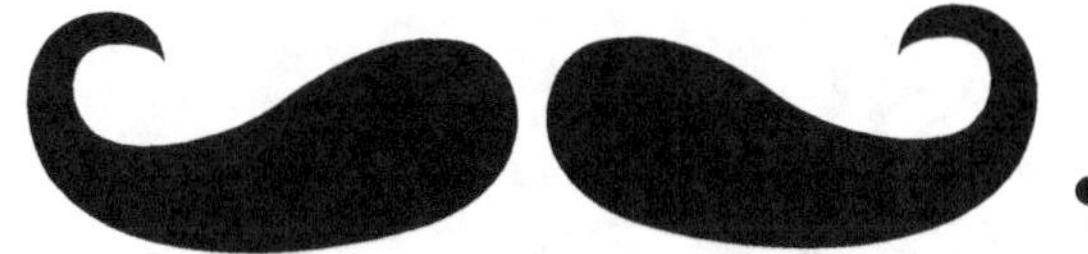

YESTERDAY I ACCIDENTALLY SWALLOWED SOME FOOD COLOURING.

THE DOCTOR SAYS I'M OK, BUT I FEEL LIKE I'VE DYED A LITTLE INSIDE.

WHICH STATE HAS THE MOST STREETS?
RHODE ISLAND.

DID YOU HEAR ABOUT THE CLAUSTROPHOBIC ASTRONAUT?

HE JUST WANTED A BIT MORE SPACE.

WHAT DO YOU CALL A MAC 'N' CHEESE THAT GETS ALL UP IN YOUR FACE?

TOO CLOSE FOR COMFORT FOOD!

Q: WHAT DID SANTA ASK RUDOLPH WHEN HE WANTED TO ASK ABOUT THE CONDITION OF THE WEATHER?

A: HE ASKED, "DO YOU THINK IT WILL RAIN, DEAR?"

A SANDWICH WALKS INTO A BAR. THE BARMAN SAYS:

'SORRY WE DON'T SERVE FOOD HERE'

A FRIEND OF MINE DIDN'T PAY HIS EXORCIST. HE GOT REPOSSESSED

I HAVE A CLEAN CONSCIOUS IT'S NEVER BEEN USED.

I ATE A CLOCK THE OTHER DAY. IT WAS VERY TIME CONSUMING.

I'D TELL YOU A CHEMISTRY JOKE BUT I KNOW I WOULDN'T GET A REACTION.

WHAT DID THE BEAVER SAY
WHEN IT SAW THE
CHRISTMAS TREE?

IT SAID,
"NICE GNAWING YOU."

HAVE YOU HEARD THE
JOKE ABOUT THE BUTTER?

I BETTER NOT TELL YOU,
IT MIGHT SPREAD!

WHAT DO ALL THE REINDEERS HANG
ON THE CHRISTMAS TREES AT
THEIR HOME?

THE HORN-AMENTS.

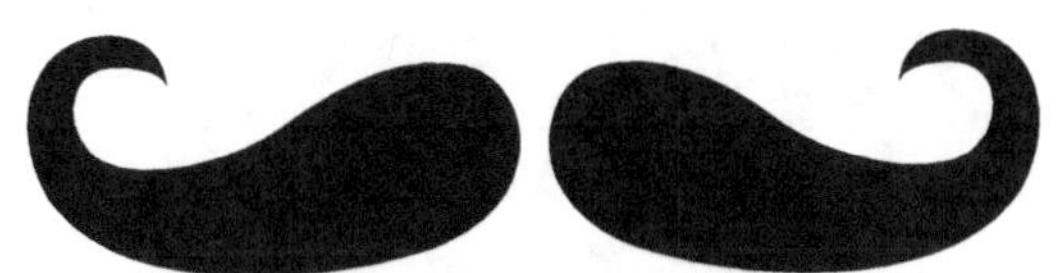

WHY DID THE GRINCH DECIDE TO GO
TO THE HAUNTED HOUSE
THE OTHER DAY?

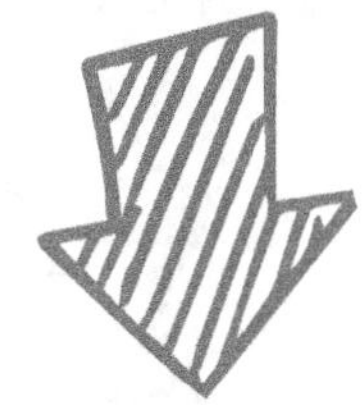

BECAUSE HE WAS SEARCHING
FOR THE HOLIDAY SPIRIT.

WHAT DID THE OCEAN SAY TO THE SAND?

NOTHING
IT JUST WAVED.

WHY DID THE ORANGE LOSE
THE RACE?

IT RAN OUT OF JUICE.

STOP LOOKING FOR THE PERFECT
MATCH;

USE A LIGHTER.

Q: WHAT SOUND DOES A WITCH'S CAR MAKE?

A: BROOM BROOM!

Q: DID YOU HEAR ABOUT THE GIRL WHO QUIT HER JOB AT THE DOUGHNUT FACTORY?

A: SHE WAS FED UP WITH THE HOLE BUSINESS.

DID YOU HEARD ABOUT THE GIANT
THAT THREW UP?
IT'S ALL OVER TOWN!

I SLEPT LIKE A LOG LAST NIGHT.
WOKE UP IN THE FIREPLACE!

MY IQ TEST RESULTS CAME BACK.
THEY WERE NEGATIVE.

TWO CANNIBALS ARE EATING A CLOWN.
ONE SAYS TO THE OTHER
DOES THIS TASTE FUNNY TO YOU?'

HOW DID SCROOGE WIN THE FOOTBALL GAME?
BECAUSE THE GHOST OF CHRISTMAS PASSED.
I STAYED UP ALL NIGHT WONDERING WHERE THE SUN WENT
THEN IT DAWNED ON ME.

HOW DO YOU MAKE HOLY WATER?

YOU BOIL THE HELL OUT OF IT.

DID YOU HEAR ABOUT THE GUY WHO HAD HIS LEFT SIDE CUT OFF?

HE'S ALL RIGHT NOW!

WHAT DOES THE STORK DO ONCE HE'S DELIVERED THE BABY?

HE LIES ON THE COUCH AND DRINKS A BEER!

I HATED FACIAL HAIR BUT THEN

IT GREW ON ME.

I'M READING AN ANTI-GRAVITY BOOK.

I CAN'T PUT IT DOWN!

Q: WHAT HAS EARS BUT CANNOT HEAR?

A: A CORNFIELD!

Q: HAVE YOU HEARD OF A MUSIC GROUP CALLED CELLOPHANE?

A: THEY MAINLY WRAP.

I WAS GOING
TO TELL A TIME-TRAVELING
JOKE, BUT YOU GUYS DIDN'T LIKE IT.

Q: WHAT KIND OF CAR DOES A SHEEP LIKE
TO DRIVE?

A: A LAMBORGHINI.

Q: WHAT DID THE ACCOUNTANT SAY WHILE
AUDITING A DOCUMENT?

A: THIS IS TAXING.

Q: WHAT DID THE JUICER SAY TO THE
ORANGE DURING SELF-QUARANTINE?

A: CAN'T WAIT TO SQUEEZE YOU!

WHY WAS
AFRAID OF   ?

BECAUSE
ATE NINE

WHAT DID THE FISH SAY
WHEN IT SWAM INTO A WALL?

DAMN!

I'M SO GOOD AT SLEEPING THAT

I DO IT WITH MY EYES CLOSED.

I SPENT A LOT OF TIME, MONEY, AND EFFORTCHILDPROOFING MY HOUSE...

BUT THE KIDS STILL GET IN.

WHAT KIND OF
JEWELRY DO
RABBITS WEAR?

CARROT GOLD.

WHAT'S THE BEST THING ABOUT
SWITZERLAND?

I DON'T KNOW, BUT THE FLAG
IS A BIG PLUS.

WHAT'S BROWN AND STICKY?

A STICK.

Q: WHY DID THE BEDDING HIDE THEIR RELATIONSHIP?

A: THEY JUST WANTED SOMETHING PILLOW-KEY!

Q: HOW MANY PARANOIDS DOES IT TAKE TO CHANGE A LIGHT BULB?

A: WHO WANTS TO KNOW?

WHAT IS THE BEST CHRISTMAS PRESENT YOU CAN GET ANYONE? A BROKEN DRUM BECAUSE YOU JUST CAN'T BEAT IT.

I TOLD MY DOCTOR I HEARD BUZZING, BUT SHE SAID IT'S JUST A BUG THAT'S GOING AROUND.

ALL VAMPIRES KEEP THEIR MONEY IN A SPECIAL PLACE THE BLOOD BANK.

Q: WHEN DOES A JOKE TURN INTO A DAD JOKE?

A: WHEN IT BECOMES APPARENT.

WHY DID THE BABY STRAWBERRY CRY?
HIS PARENTS WERE IN A JAM.
WHY DID THE SCARECROW WIN AN AWARD?
BECAUSE HE WAS OUTSTANDING IN HIS FIELD

WHAT DO THE ELVES POST ON SOCIAL MEDIA WHEN THEY GO SOME PLACE NICE?

THEIR ELF-IES.

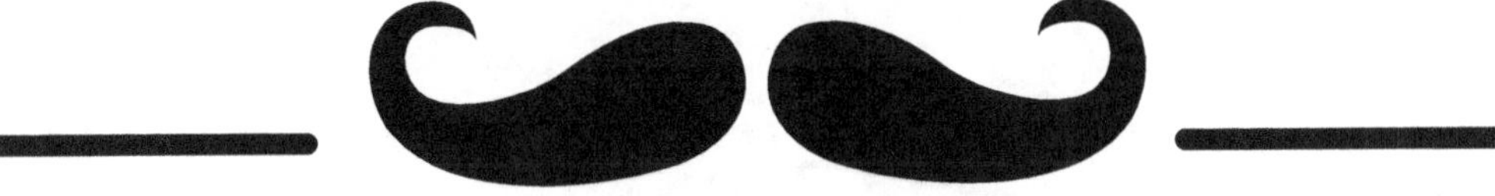

CAN I WATCH TV?

YES BUT DON'T TURN IT ON.

WHY DID THE PHOTO GO TO JAIL?

IT WAS FRAMED.

WHY DID THE OLD MAN FALL IN
THE WELL?

BECAUSE HE COULDN'T SEE
THAT WELL!

CAN FEBRUARY MARCH?

NO, BUT APRIL MAY!

Q: WHAT DID THE EVIL CHICKEN LAY?

A: DEVILED EGGS.

Q: WHY DID THE MAN NAME HIS DOGS ROLEX AND TIMEX?

A: BECAUSE THEY WERE WATCH DOGS.

GHOSTS ARE BAD LIARS BECAUSE YOU CAN SEE RIGHT THROUGH THEM.

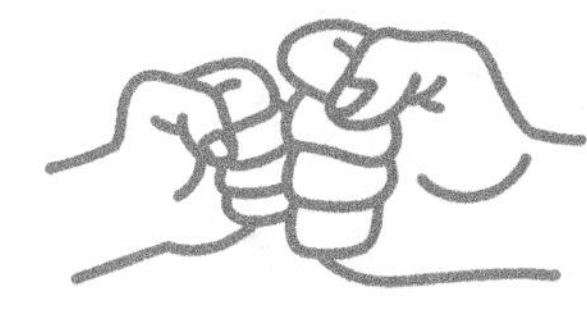

I ONCE WROTE A SONG ABOUT A TORTILLA, BUT IT'S MORE OF A WRAP.

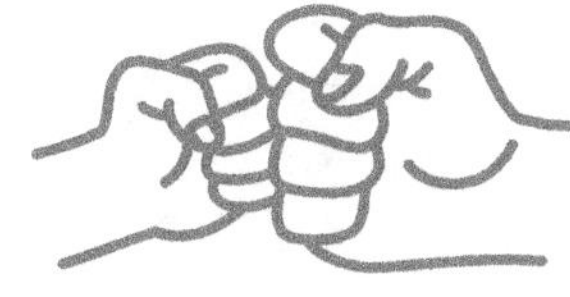

IF TWO VEGETARIANS GET IN AN ARGUMENT, IS IT STILL CALLED BEEF?

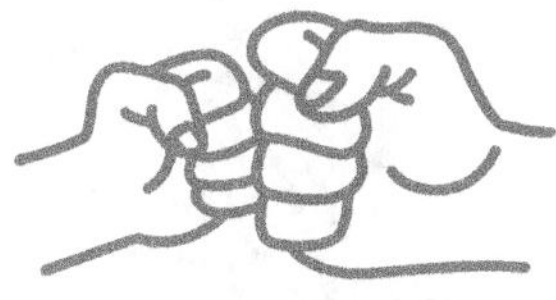

WHAT DO THE LITTLE HELPERS OF SANTA LEARN WHEN THEY FIRST GO TO SCHOOL? THEY LEARN THE ELF-ABETS.

WHY DO MELONS HAVE WEDDINGS?

THEY CANTALOUPE.

WHY DIDN'T THE SKELETON CROSS THE ROAD?

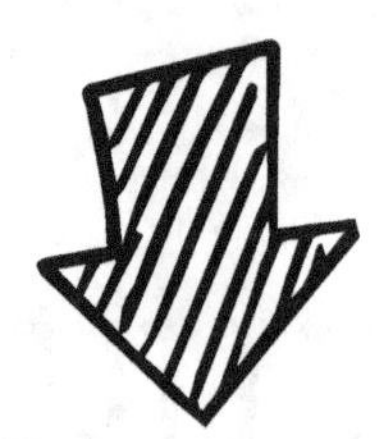

BECAUSE HE HAD NO GUTS!

I WASN'T GOING TO GET A BRAIN TRANSPLANT.

BUT THEN I CHANGED MY MIND.

I READ THAT BY LAW YOU MUST TURN ON YOUR HEADLIGHTS WHEN IT'S RAINING IN SWEDEN, BUT HOW AM I SUPPOSED TO KNOW WHEN IT IS RAINING IN SWEDEN?

WHY CAN'T A NOSE BE INCHES LONG?

THEN IT'D BE A FOOT.

MY WIFE SAID I WAS IMMATURE.

SO I TOLD HER TO GET OUT
OF MY FORT.

DO YOU KNOW THE LAST THING MY
GRANDFATHER SAID TO ME
BEFORE HE KICKED THE BUCKET?

"GRANDSON, WATCH HOW FAR
I CAN KICK THIS BUCKET."

Q: DID YOU HEAR THEY ARRESTED THE DEVIL?

A: YEAH, THEY GOT HIM ON POSSESSION.

Q: WHAT WOULD YOU CALL A KID THAT DOESN'T BELIEVE IN SANTA CLAUS?

A: HE'D BE CALLED THE REBEL WITHOUT A CLAUS.

SHOULDN'T THE "ROOF" OF YOUR MOUTH ACTUALLY BE CALLED THE CEILING?

WHAT'S THE FAVORITE CHRISTMAS CAROL OF EVERY NEW PARENT? SILENT NIGHT.

DOGS CAN'T OPERATE MRI MACHINES BUT CATSCAN.

WHAT ARE THE BEST CHRISTMAS SWEATERS MADE FROM?

FLEECE NAVIDAD.

WHAT DO YOU CALL A SLEEPING BULL?
A BULLDOZER.
WHAT DO YOU CALL AN UNPREDICTABLE CAMERA?
A LOOSE CANON.

WHERE DO SANTA AND HIS REINDEERS STOP FOR COFFEE IN BETWEEN THEIR JOURNEY?

THEY GO TO STAR-BUCKS.

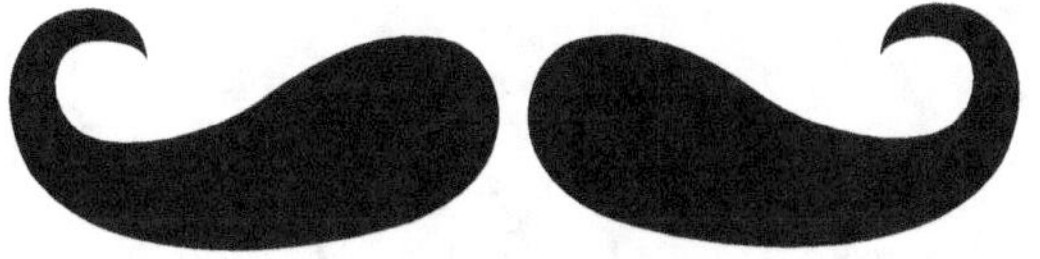

WHAT IS THE DIFFERENCE BETWEEN AN ANGRY CIRCUS OWNER AND A ROMAN BARBER?

ONE IS A RAVING SHOWMAN, THE OTHER IS A SHAVING ROMAN.

WHY DID THE SCARECROW WIN AN AWARD?

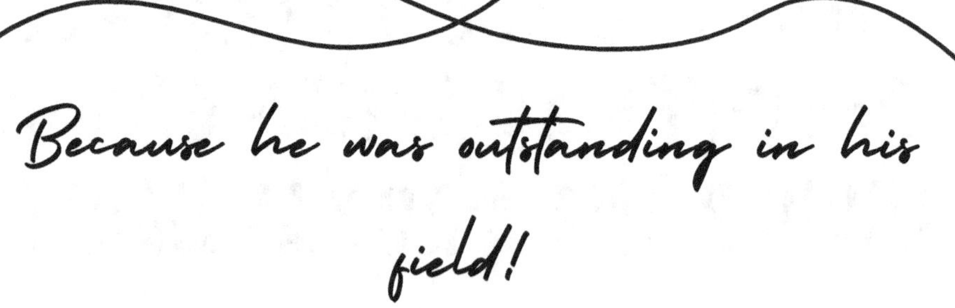

Because he was outstanding in his field!

DID YOU HEAR ABOUT THE MATHEMATICIAN WHO'S AFRAID OF NEGATIVE NUMBERS?

He'll stop at nothing to avoid them.

WHAT DO YOU CALL FAKE SPAGHETTI?

An impasta.

HOW DOES A PENGUIN BUILD ITS HOUSE?

Igloos it together!

WHAT DO YOU GET WHEN YOU CROSS A SNOWMAN AND A VAMPIRE?

frostbite

WHY DON'T SCIENTISTS TRUST ATOMS?

Because they make up everything!

WHY COULDN`T THE BICYCLE STAND UP BY ITSELF?

WHAT`S BROWN AND STICKY?

A stick.

HOW DOES A SNOWMAN GET AROUND?

By riding an "icicle."

WHAT DO YOU CALL CHEESE THAT ISN'T YOURS?

Nacho cheese.

WHAT DID ONE HAT SAY TO THE OTHER?

Stay here; I'm going on ahead!

WHAT DO YOU CALL A FISH WEARING A BOWTIE?

HOW DO YOU ORGANIZE A SPACE PARTY?

You planet.

WHY DID THE GOLFER BRING TWO PAIRS OF PANTS?

In case he got a hole in one.

WHY DON'T OYSTERS DONATE TO CHARITY?

Because they are shellfish.

WHY DID THE COFFEE FILE A POLICE REPORT?

It got mugged.

WHAT DO YOU CALL A FACTORY THAT MAKES GOOD PRODUCTS?

A satisfactory.

WHAT DID THE GRAPE DO WHEN IT GOT STEPPED ON?

Nothing, but it let out a little wine.

WHY DON'T SKELETONS FIGHT EACH OTHER?

They don't have the guts.

WHAT DO YOU CALL A SNOWMAN WITH A SIX-PACK?

An abdominal snowman.

WHAT DO YOU CALL A PILE OF CATS?

A meowtain.

WHY DO CHICKEN COOPS ONLY HAVE TWO DOORS?

Because if they had four, they'd be a chicken sedan.

WHAT DID THE JANITOR SAY WHEN HE JUMPED OUT OF THE CLOSET?

Supplies!

WHY DID THE TOMATO TURN RED?

Because it saw the salad dressing!

WHY DID THE MATH BOOK LOOK SAD?

Because it had too many problems.

HOW DO YOU CATCH A SQUIRREL?

Climb a tree and act like a nut!

WHAT DID THE GRAPE SAY WHEN IT GOT STEPPED ON?

Nothing, it just let out a little wine.

HOW DO YOU MAKE A TISSUE DANCE?

You put a little boogie in it!

WHY DID THE SCARECROW BECOME A SUCCESSFUL POLITICIAN?

Because he was outstanding in his field!

WHY DID THE SCARECROW BECOME A SUCCESSFUL POLITICIAN?

Because he was outstanding in his field!

WHY DID THE COMPUTER GO TO THERAPY?

It had too many bytes of emotional baggage

WHAT'S A VAMPIRE'S FAVORITE FRUIT?

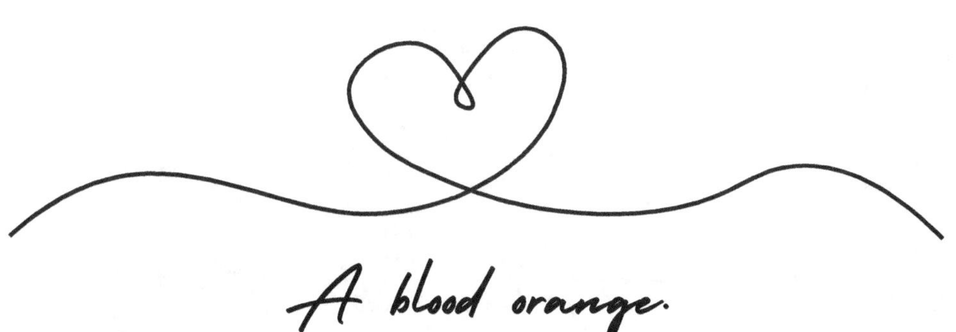

A blood orange.

HOW DOES A PENGUIN BUILD ITS WEBSITE?

Igloos it together with HTML.

WHAT DO YOU CALL A FISH WITH NO EYES

I TOLD MY WIFE SHE WAS DRAWING HER EYEBROWS TOO HIGH

She looked surprised.

PARALLEL LINES HAVE SO MUCH IN COMMON.

It's a shame they'll never meet.

WHAT`S ORANGE AND SOUNDS LIKE A PARROT?

A carrot.

WHAT`S ORANGE AND SOUNDS LIKE A PARROT?

A carrot.

I TOLD MY COMPUTER
I NEEDED A BREAK

and now it won't stop sending me vacation ads.

I TOLD MY COMPUTER I NEEDED A BREAK

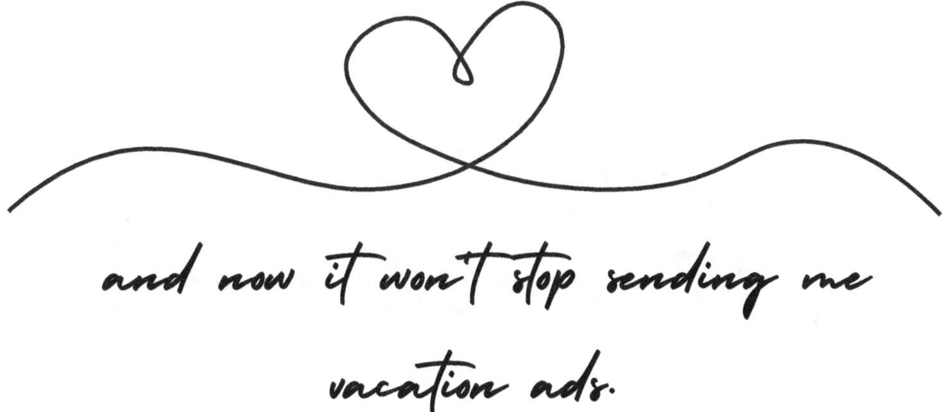

WHAT DID ONE OCEAN SAY TO THE OTHER OCEAN?

Nothing, they just waved.

WHY DID THE CHICKEN JOIN A BAND?

Because it had the drumsticks.

WHY DID THE CHICKEN JOIN A BAND?

Because it had the drumsticks.

HOW DO YOU ORGANIZE A FANTASTIC PARTY FOR COWS?

You moooove and groove.

WHAT DID ONE PLATE SAY TO ANOTHER PLATE?

"Tonight, dinner's on me!"

WHAT KIND OF TREE FITS IN YOUR HAND?

A palm tree.

HOW DO YOU MAKE A TISSUE DANCE?

You put a little boogie in it!

WHY DID THE COOKIE GO TO THE DOCTOR?

It was feeling crumbly.

WHAT DO YOU CALL A BEAR WITH NO TEETH?

A gummy bear.

WHY DID THE BANANA GO TO THE DOCTOR?

It wasn't peeling well.

WHAT DID ONE WALL SAY TO THE OTHER WALL?

"I'll meet you at the corner!"

WHAT DO YOU CALL A COW WITH NO LEGS?

Ground beef.

WHAT DO YOU CALL A SLEEPING BULL?

A bulldozer.

WHY DON'T SEAGULLS FLY OVER THE BAY?

Because then they'd be bagels.

HOW DO YOU MAKE A LEMON DROP?

Just let it fall.

WHAT DO YOU CALL A COW WITH A SENSE OF HUMOR?

Laughing stock.

WHY DID THE COMPUTER CATCH A COLD?

It had a virus.

WHAT'S A PIRATE'S FAVORITE LETTER?

Arrr! (You might think it's 'R,' but it's really the 'C' they love.)

WHAT DID ONE WALL SAY TO THE OTHER WALL?

"I'll meet you at the corner!"

WHAT DID THE BABY CORN SAY TO THE MAMA CORN?

"Where's popcorn?"